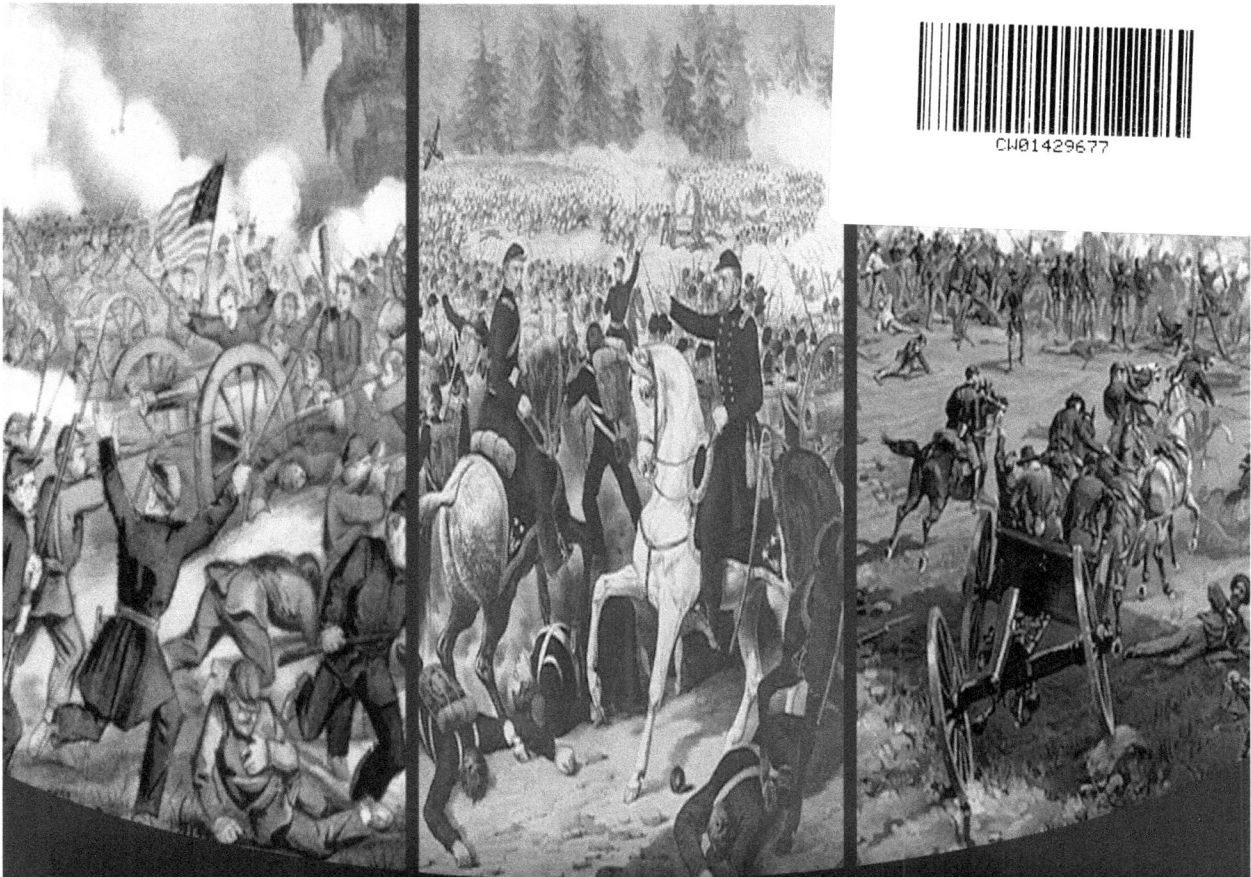

BATTLE OF GETTYSBURG

A BRIEF HISTORY FROM BEGINNING TO END

HISTORY HUB

Bonus Downloads

*Get Free Books with **Any Purchase**History Encounters*

Every purchase comes with a FREE download!

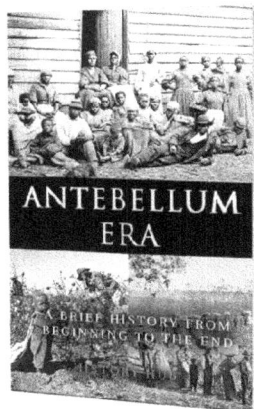

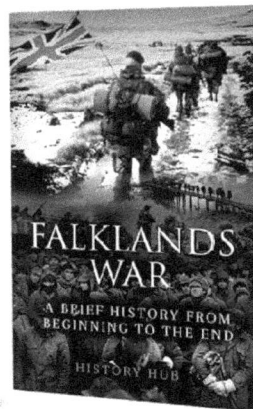

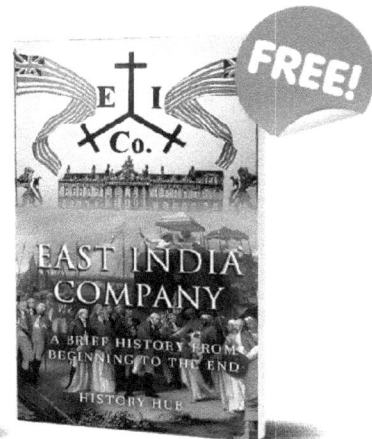

Battle at Gettysburg

A Brief History from Beginning to the End

History Encounters

CONTENTS

Chapter One
Introduction

There are a lot of times that the term "turning point" has been used throughout history. Examples of these events are – and are not limited to - The Fall of Constantinople, The Fall of the Berlin Wall, and Walking on the Moon. But there is one "turning point" in American history that is still talked about, raises some controversy, and is romanticized through media and culture. This event is the Battle of Gettysburg. This battle took place in America during the Civil War; this historic occasion lasted for three days.

The battle of Gettysburg was short but essential; it was a "costly battle," as a lot of historians would say, because of the casualties that occurred during the time. The battle was on American soil, fought by divided Americans. Back in the Civil War, the Americans were divided between the Confederates, who were characterized as the states who separated themselves from the Union (the other states) primarily due to their beliefs on slavery which resulted in their different economic policies and their priorities. The other side is called the Unions, who were against slavery and focused mainly on industrialization, specifically their transportation and communication systems.

The leader of the Confederate Army was Robert Lee, while the leader of the Union Army was Ulysses Grant. The way they met on the battlefield of Gettysburg was actually not intentional. They just collided with each other by accident – a classic example of "wrong place, wrong time." But even if they did it by accident or not, they still fought, and the battle turned the tides in the Union's favor. On July 1, the first day of the fight, it seemed like the Confederates would win this battle. However, the Union built a solid defensive line, and that allowed them to hold their own on the second day, and on the third and final day, they won the battle. But note that even if they won that battle, that did not end the war. It took them a few years to win the war across the United States. Although, the fight at Gettysburg did help them reach that ending a bit faster.

When looking at the battle of Gettysburg, you must look through different views. This is so because this was a military event, and there are so many factors to see with varying sets of eyes. Looking at it from a military geologist's watch will make you see the importance of Gettysburg's terrain and how it was able to help the Union and Confederate armies plan their offensive and defensive strikes. If you look at it through the eyes of the soldiers who were actually part of the battle, you would see how one could be proud of that moment – that moment when their men went in bravely for their cause. And if you look at the war through the eyes of civilians, specifically the women, and what they were experiencing during that time, you would see the similarities and differences in their experiences.

People see the story of the Battle of Gettysburg, and they don't all think the same thought immediately. Some people remember it as a battle between two opposing forces, divided by their beliefs on slavery. At the same time, other people see it as a sight for remembrance and hope. This is caused by how some have already romanticized the battle of Gettysburg, making it the source of inspiration for books and movies. Some would think this is wrong, but some believe it is alright since the story of Gettysburg is still told, even though it is perceived differently.

Now, one of the most memorable moments that the battle of Gettysburg was able to produce was Lincoln's address. We all know the beginning of it: "Four scores and seven years ago..." And it is memorable because of the message it gave. The day that Lincoln gave his speech was also during the ceremony where they consecrated the cemetery, giving the fallen soldiers the respect and gratitude they deserved. Many people were invited to this event, including the surviving soldiers from the war.

Knowing all this is essential. But before you go into the details of remembering Gettysburg and seeing it from different perspectives, you must first read how it happened in a narrative and chronological manner. You must also know the clear divide between the Confederates and the Union and how their divide came to be.

Chapter Two
Confederates and Union

When the Southern states of South Carolina, Mississippi, Florida, Alabama, Georgia, Louisiana, Texas, Virginia, Arkansas, Tennessee, and North Carolina all separated themselves from the Union in 1860–1861, it caused a riot of armed hostilities throughout the decades of sectional tension over slavery. Between the years of 1815 to 1961, the economy of the Northern states was continuously modernizing and diversifying. The Northerners continued to rely on free labor and seriously invested in revolutionizing their transportation systems and communication networks. When compared to the Southern states, their economy mainly consisted of large farms that relied heavily on the labor force – in other terms: slavery. Instead of investing in aspects like what the Northerners did, they zeroed in on their labor force.

The expansion of slavery into new states has been a problem ever since the Northwest Ordinance of 1784. They found a sort of stable ground when they made the Missouri Compromise of 1820. However, this resulted in a string of political arguments about slavery. The states of the North wanted to protect free labor, and it became all too real by the 1850s. At the same time, the states of the South had a fear that if they stopped the expansion of slavery would mean them losing power. Throughout the decade, their divide became more and more evident. When Abraham Lincoln came into the picture, explicitly calling out the end to slavery, the seven southern states (mentioned at the start) separated themselves. They continued to what they believed in slavery and became the Confederates. After the secession, there were 23 states that remained in the Union.

Chapter Three
The Campaign

General Robert Lee, the leader of the Confederate Army, planned his campaign for the battle in a similar template as he did when he ended the battle of Antietam in September 1862. After that, he gave emphasis on the importance of destroying the bridge over the Susquehanna River at Harrisburg and the need to disable the Pennsylvania Railroad so that they could put a stop to communication with the west.

When General Lee was injured at Chancellorsville, his troops had to reorganize themselves. Now, the infantry corps were under the leadership of Longstreet, Hill, and Eswell, while Stuart spearheaded the cavalry division.

The Confederates started to move on June 3 from Fredericksburg to Blue Ridge up until Shenandoah Valley. On June 9, there was a battle at Brandy Station where Union horsemen were finally on equal ground with the Confederate cavalry. However, the Confederates continued on their way to Pennsylvania. On June 28, Hill and Longstreet arrived at Chambersburg, which was just 16 miles out from the northern part of Pennsylvania. Eswell's corps stayed at Carlisle on June 27.

Something happened between June 25 and June 28, and something unexpected happened. The cavalry battle between Stuart and Pleasanton (Union) at Brandy Station convinced General Joseph Hooker, who then led the Union Army, that the Confederates were moving northward. Upon hearing this, Lincoln and General Halleck ordered Hooker to go north and keep the Confederates at bay there to Washington.

General Stuart, the commander of the Confederate Cavalry, got approval from General Lee to work against the rear of the Union army as they went northward.

Chapter Four
Day One

While the Confederate Army division of Heth arrived at Cashtown on June 29, Pettigrew's men were sent to give them supplies by going through Gettysburg. However, Pettigrew's brigade was not able to penetrate the Union's cavalry, so they went back to Cashtown. When General Meade of the Union forces was given the commander position, he moved his troops to the north. He gave his engineers clear instructions to canvas the defensive battle position at Pipe Creek near Taneytown in the northern part of Maryland. Buford's confederate cavalry was then made to have surveillance at the Gettysburg area. None of them figured that Gettysburg would be the field where the battle would commence.

Hill, while Lee was still absent, took charge. On the crack of dawn of July 1, he ordered his men, the people in Archer and

Davis's division (under Heth), to go take Chambersburg Road to enter Gettysburg. He did this as a test run, checking the strength and resilience of the Union's Forces. As his test subjects pushed through to Marsh Creek, which is 4 miles from the Gettysburg line, they were ambushed by the Union cavalry. While this was happening, Buford's Confederate division of cavalry had positioned themselves to the southwest of Gettysburg to McPherson Ridge, just a mile from Gettysburg.

The morning of July 1 kept getting longer; the brigades of Archer and Davis, who were left on Chambersburg Road, were sent to Herr Ridge, with Pegram's artillery's support, then were able to charge across Willoughby Run. The Union cavalry, of course, had the upper hand in their rapid-fire. As they dismounted and fought with their men on the ground, they were able to defend themselves from Heth's men. Around ten in the morning, aid arrived at the Union army with General John F.

Reynolds' first Infantry corps. They came in from the Seminary Ridge.

The battle continued on, everyone fighting so hard. By the time the Confederate's Archers came into the picture, the Confederates had a new burst of energy as they attacked across Willoughby Run, while the Union army, Meredith's Iron Brigade specifically, struck at the flank of the Confederates,

The Battle of Oak Ridge. Even though there was a battle all around Gettysburg, the main bulk of the two armies were fighting it over a place Buford, a Confederate, picked. The Confederates under Rodes received orders to go to Gettysburg. The Confederates strategically used the wooded ridge as a protective shield from the Union Cavalry north of Gettysburg. At around one in the afternoon, Rodes brought out his gun as they positioned themselves at Oak Ridge and opened fire at General Abner Doubleday of the Union Army. Doubleday saw this and quickly shifted strategies, turning his lines towards the northeast to meet the Confederates on Oak Ridge. As the Confederates gave it their all, so did the Unions. Iverson, a Confederate, and his men were almost all killed. The Union troops just kept on piling up as more of them came into the picture.

Dole's Confederate brigade charged through until he was able to force some Union troops backward for just a moment. But that was all they needed to regain their momentum because it rendered the Union's position on the north of Gettysburg almost defenseless. As the day continued on, the Union army was standing their ground, that is until there was a big hit from the Confederate's artillery and infantry. Barlow of the Union was gravely hit. Soon enough, the Union forces scattered. However, the Union men on Oak Ridge continued their battle against Doles, even though they were already at a disadvantage with their other men being broken down by the Confederates.

When the Union army retreated from the battle on the evening of July 1, they quickly set up their defensive positions at Cemetery Hill, Culp's Hill, and a part of Cemetery Ridge. The Union's right flank was left to be consolidated when Slocum arrived through the Baltimore Pike and Sickles through the Emmitsburg Road. This made them have a solid defensive battle line in the shape of a fish hook that is 3 miles long. They also had the advantage of high ground and interior lines.

General Meade of the Confederates, who was in Taneytown, had just got informed that another battle was developing, and Reynolds was killed. A considerable chunk of his army was within 5 miles of Gettysburg, so Meade sent General Hancock to canvas, investigate, and report the situation to him. Hancock was able to reach the field just as the Union Army was falling back to make a defensive line on Cemetery Hill. Meade then made a decision to isolate the Union forces where they were. On Day 1, the Confederates seemed to be winning this battle.

Chapter Five
Day Two

The Confederate Order of Longstreet was to take position across Emmitsburg Road and, once ready, attack the left flank of the Union line on Cemetery Ridge. He used the Herr Ridge to be his shield from the Union's signallers' eyes as he marched from Chambersburg Road to the west of Gettysburg. Once he marched through to the Black Horse Tavern on Fairfield Road, he only then noticed that his men were in the line of sight of the Unions and began to retrace his course, using the trees this time as the screen. Longstreet and his troop went through Willoughby Run Valley to get into position at Emmitsburg Road at around 3:30 in the afternoon. Right away, Longstreet spotted Sickles' defensive barriers lined on the Peach Orchard and along Emmitsburg Road. Colonel Alexander of the Confederates ordered

Longstreet's artillery battalion to use their full force toward the Union's defensive lines.

After seeing the defensive lines of the Union, General Warren, Meade's Chief of Engineers, went to the crest of Little Round Top and found an unoccupied hill, if you don't count the signal station. Warren got news from the signal men that they thought Confederate troops could be shielded from the Union's view through the wooded ridge a mile to the west. Smith, a confederate, knowing this, commanded his men to open fire into the woods.

Once this happened, Sykes' Union Fifth Corps started to go across the Cemetery Ridge towards the front. Warren, who was in need of support, received it from the brigades of Vincent and Weed, who ran from the Little Round Top. Law's troops started to rise from Hill's south slope while Weed's Union brigade crossed the crest and fought with the Robertson's Texans on the west slope. Hazlett's Confederate battery then blew, and hand-to-hand combat started. Weed and Hazlett were killed while Vincent was injured.

However, the battle continued on the Little Round Top with Robertson's Confederate men and Law's Union army. The battle was long, and it lasted for four hours; the defensive line created by the Unions was gone. However, the Union line on Cemetery Ridge is still stable and standing.

The Confederate's plan was not over just yet. Eswell was directed to attack the left of Cemetery Hill and Culp's Hill. When dusk fell, after the artillery fire had stopped, Johnson from the Confederates and his men charged at the Union army who were stationed at Culp's Hill. However, he failed to conquer because of the steep incline of the Hill and the power the Unions had. The Unions on Culp's Hill were not strong in numbers, though, and the Geary and Ruger forces were asked to fortify the Hill around an hour before Eswell's attack on them.

While Johnson attacked the Union at Culp's Hill, Early's Confederate Infantry attacked the East wing of Cemetery Hill. The attack reached all the way to the crest of the Hill, which resulted in another hand-to-hand combat. However, Rodes' failure to move out of the Gettysburg streets and the attack on the Hill from the west led by Hancock caused Early to retreat. It was the nighttime that ended day 2 of the battle at Gettysburg.

On Day 2, the Union was steady as a rock.

Chapter Six
Day Three

Meade was convinced that the Confederates would attack from the left side of their defensive lines. So, he placed his strong forces at that side, with Hancock's forces holding the center. General Hunt, who was the chief of Artillery in the Union Army, brought up weapons to replace their used ones. As these plans behind the battlegrounds were happening, Ruger and Lockwood's men were sent to reoccupy the grounds. However, Geary, a soldier who misunderstood the orders, led the men to Baltimore Pike. Here, they overheard scouts talking about how the south of Culp's Hill and Spangler's Spring had been now occupied by the Confederates. Hearing this, Ruger planned an attack at dawn; he rallied his forces along with Pike with the new artillery units at their disposal.

As the sun rose on July 3, the Union army had their guns ready at Baltimore Pike and started to rain down on Johnson's Confederates, who were at Spangler's Spring. Because of the terrain, the number of trees prevented the Confederates from responding to fire. The Union skirmishers started to disperse and ambush the Confederate camps. On that day, the Confederates took in a heavy attack for a long time.

By the time it was 10 AM, Ruger had thought that a flank attack would be the best next move to do. He believed that it would break any resistance the Confederates had left. So Ruger ordered Colonel Silas Colgrove to launch an attack on the Confederate's left flank. Even though fire slowed them down, it did not stop them. However, their attack was a failure because the Confederates had a firm hold on their left flank. While this was happening, Ruger's and Geary's end was succeeding so much so that the Confederates were retreating back to Rock Creek, which was out of shooting range. By the time it was 11 in the morning, the Union troops were still in line to become victorious.

General Meade was able to formulate a plan of defense by late morning of July 3. The only problem for him now was where the next Confederate attack would occur. General Hunt suggests placing strong battery lines as a defense on the crest of Cemetery Ridge. As for their final preparation, Meade checked his men at the Stone Wall before heading southward to Little Round Top.

Meade was not the only one making plans at that time. Lee finally came back and organized his own plans for the Confederates. He was planning attack formations on Seminary Ridge since he planned on attacking the Union Army at their center. Lee ordered the rearrangement of the batteries to help his plan come true. By noon, there were around 140 guns in the line from Peach Orchard all the way to the north, where the Seminary buildings are.

Focusing now on the west of Emmitsburg Road, where the terrain allows them to hide in plain sight from the Union lines, General George Pickett's three brigades are stationed there. These three brigades are Kemper, Armistead, and Garnett. And General Stuart, who had lost touch with Lee, was ordered to take a position on the Confederate left.

Now the battlefield has been set up, and it is time for the final battle to begin.

Are You Enjoying Reading?

As an independent publisher

with a tiny marketing budget

we rely on readers, like you.

If you're receiving help from this book,

would you please take a moment to write a brief review?

We really appreciate it.

Chapter Seven

Final Battle

At one in the afternoon, the guns of Miller's battery started to open fire in rapid succession. The Union gunners who were stationed on Cemetery Ridge waited before attacking, wanting to see where the Confederate batteries were stationed. For almost two hours, the firepower duel continued until the Union's fire went a bit limp. Hunt had to announce a partial cessation so that they could cool down the guns and conserve ammunition.

The Union men who were by the Stone Wall were momentarily hidden from the Confederates due to the amount of smoke that surrounded them. However, the Confederates on the Little Round Top could see beyond the smoke, and they coached the Confederates on the ground, telling them where to go. Pickett ordered them to go to the left after finding his brigade again. On the other hand, Kemper was going in from the south of the Codori building, and Garnett and Armistead were going in from the north.

Pickett had a feeling that the Union army had a strong position in their artillery and infantry by the stone walls on the ridge, but it was too late. The Union guns, which were at the far south near Little Round Top, along with the others on Cemetery Hill, opened fire from both the left and right flanks. While Pickett's men continued to go through the Union, the Union used their strategic moves. The Confederate lines were both crumbling and reforming again and again under the Union's attacks.

In the end, the power of the Union horsemen was so well coordinated that it stopped the slaughter of Struat's men. After almost three hours of battle, the Confederates surrendered and went back north of Gettysburg. The Union horsemen then stood their ground and successfully squashed any hope of the Confederate cavalry coming back to fight again.

On July 3, the battle ended, and Lee decided to make the Confederates retreat. The Unions have won.

This is a picture of Union Soldiers marching to battle.

This is a monument to the Confederate Soldiers.

Chapter Eight
Military Geological View

During the early 1960s, geologists have been trying to study the role of Gettysburg's terrain during the battle back in the Civil War. The geologists want to investigate the military strategies made, to understand how the geology of Gettysburg fits in the picture.

The Town of Gettysburg is on a Triassic sedimentary rift basin in the Piedmont east of the Valley and Ridge and the Blue Ridge provinces. This land is filled to the brim with shales and sandstones of the Gettysburg Formation, which struck the southwest-northeast. It is important to note that these sedimentary rocks were intruded during the Jurassic by diabase sills and dykes. The York Haven Diabase formed the prominent hills south of Gettysburg, such as Cemetery Ridge, Culp's Hill, and Little Round Tops. As for the dykes of the younger Rossville, Diabase created the Seminary Ridge.

The intrusion of the York Haven Diabase has been associated with the shale's significant hornfels, comprising the Gettysburg formation. This means that the outcrop pattern created the "fishhook" that helped the Union win this battle.

Andrew Brown of the Pennsylvania State Geological Survey made one of the first significant studies that emphasized this. Brown was able to publish his article regarding this topic under the title "Geology and the Battle of Gettysburg." His study showed his examination of the campaign that paved the way to the battle, what the movements of the Union Armies from the south were like and what the progression of the Confederates was like in the north. General Lee of the Confederates had the plan to invade the north to take the current battle away from Virginia and intimidate the Union in their land. Brown saw that Lee's invasion plan was to use the topography of Blue Ridge to shield his troops from the Union's men, at least in Virginia. Harold Winters also saw this view; he was saying that the definite structural land of the northeast or southwest along the Valley and Ridge province was able to create a north-south path for movements. However, it constrained the east-west movements and paved the way to a series of gaps in the Blue Ridge Mountains that was created by a drainage capture to the Shenandoah River.

Brown did not stop there, and he continued his study. In the last few years of it, members from the Pennsylvania Survey and Roger Cuffy of Pennsylvania State University helped him analyze this even more. They started to focus on the "topographic fish hook," the outcrop of diabase that was a very important defensive strategy that the Union's made during the second and last day of the battle.

The article goes on about the role of the specific areas of geology and how it influences the movement, observation, concealment, possibility of entrenchment, and supply of provisions and materials in battle.

As divided earlier, the battle at Gettysburg can be divided into three days: July 1, July 2, and July 3. From geologists' view, Day 1 (July 1) was all about going through the open and rolling terrain. The Union Troops were victorious in commanding the high ground. On Day 2 (July 2), it was all about the Confederates who wanted to gain the high-ground advantage by attacking the hills through the flanks. And on Day 3 (July 3), it was basically an assault over open ground. The low forward slant of the Union's position helped them win the war at Gettysburg.

Chapter Nine

Soldier's View: Minnesota

In the view of a military historian, Gettysburg does not have a tremendous crucial strategic importance. Yes, the battleground of the Union and Confederate armies accidentally made contact with each other on July 1. General George Meade nor General Robert Lee made the conscious decision to meet and do battle on Gettysburg soil. Even though the Union army won, it was at a cost. They were not able to fully utilize their victory, so there were still two extra years of war before Lee waved that white flag.

However, Gettysburg did turn the tide for Lee and the army of Northern Virginia. The Union Army of Potomac, which had been losing throughout the 12 months of the war, was able to stand its ground and push Lee and his confederate soldiers to retreat into Southern territory.

The battle at Gettysburg always piqued the interest of Minnesotans due to the enormous amount of bravery and the significant loss it cost the first Minnesota Regiment; they were part of the fighting during the second and third days. The immense pride the Minnesotans have was during that of the second day (July 2), the first Minnesota Regiment had a heroic charge on that day, and it was officially recorded in history and memorialized through art.

Chapter Ten

Women's View: Women of Gettysburg and the Southern Women

The women of Gettysburg shared some similarities with the women of the South. One of the similarities is the thought that they had to do "a man's business" since the men were all off at war. Although, studies show that these happened not because men decided to leave for the war but because they were forced to. Either way, both the North and south women were forced to take upon their shoulders the responsibility that men would usually be responsible for.

Another similarity between the women of Gettysburg is that the women who were part of the Confederates were that they were under military occupation. Since the Confederates did occupy most of the town, the people of Gettysburg lived in fear of the hostile forces. Fortunately enough for them, the

Confederates were not as aggressive in the areas of the North compared to the Union forces in the South.

Women in Gettysburg were also very socially conservative; this is primarily seen in the women in the Southern part of the country. This type of conservatism was, without a doubt, a reason why they refused to demand acknowledgment for their wartime service. Due to their silence during the battle, the women of Gettysburg did not have an idolization of Jennie Wade, as the whole nation has. Either way, women did not help in stopping the image of women from being known as silent and passive throughout history.

One last similarity between the South and the women of Gettysburg was the acceptance of female nursing. Gettysburg women were permitted to help in the infirmaries to heal the wounded.

Since they do have the difference in geological placement, the women of Gettysburg did have some differences from the Southern Women. The most evident distinction between the two was Gettysburg's lack of economic deprivation after the battle. The women of the North, who are known to be Confederate women, are the people who did not take the biggest hit from it. The two armies both had almost emptied their provisions – food, medical supplies, and water - yes, but the women from the South suffered the most from this economic depletion.

Another difference is that the women of the South had slavery in their system. For the people of the South, the presence of slavery is the cornerstone of their society, which the women of Gettysburg do not believe in and therefore do not have. Due to the fact that slavery was a factor In all the relationships there, the violence in their system was prominent. Whether the southern women were white or black, something remained constant with them: slavery was for all women.

Another difference between the two women of Gettysburg is that the South has this idea of "unruly women." This means that women tagged as such did not meet the high bar of expectations that people would have over "proper ladylike" women. "Unruly" women were thought to be agents of temporary change while the war was going on. It was too non-traditional, and it caused riots and divisions. However, they were unsuccessful in shifting the reality of their daily lives.

Chapter Eleven

Women's View: Women of Gettysburg and the Northern Women

Now that we have discussed comparing Gettysburg women to the south, we will discuss their similarities and differences with the northern women of America. Gettysburg women collectively share the zeal of the Northern women for a clearly defined feminine, sentimental charity. Gettysburg also shared the concept of community networks with the northern women.

Community networks were both present in the town of Gettysburg and the farms that surround the countryside. Grabbing information was much easier in the city. However, citizens who would just look out of their windows or doors would immediately see what was going on in the battle. At the same time, the people who lived on the farms had a more challenging time getting information.

The differences, though, between the Gettysburg women and the Northern women are found in the presence and function of organized generosity. The thing about Gettysburg women is that they were not as concerned with the public welfare functions of the town during battle. For example, the Poor House, which is a big dispenser of aid to the needy, was run by men throughout history. Even though women were active in some groundwork for kindness, the power of these organizations was on the men's shoulders.

Gettysburg has many known geological places, and they all played a part in the Battle. This is the Devil's Den.

This is a monument commemorating the women of Gettysburg.

Chapter Twelve
Remembering Gettysburg's History and Memory

Memory and History

The difference between Memory and History is that Memory lets the subject remember the past and provides historical knowledge in the form of a story. When it comes to the study of any history, even as big as the Battle of Gettysburg, Memory is just as important as history. People's thoughts on Gettysburg have been influenced by our history books and culture, education, society, social media, and social gatherings. These influences are not based on anything, they are rooted in myths, misinterpretations, exaggerations, and false statements from what people think happened on those three days in history.

Charles Mauer makes a quote, "Memory complements history. History corrects Memory." This quote reminds every one of the value of historical consciousness. It is essential to note the relationship between the two concepts. History needs Memory to provide content and context; however, there are times when events, such as the Battle of Gettysburg, can't rely on memories of witnesses because of the inaccuracies, myths, and misunderstandings that might have influenced their minds. Hence, even though that history is from Memory, the role of the historian is to be the last line of defense – the editor and quality control of the Memory before it is turned into recorded history.

So, you can understand the importance of popular Memory of any historical event, how Memory works, and its correlation with history. Memory is not just a link between consciousness and the past, but it is a way for humans to perceive past events. Not only does Memory set the foundation of history, but it also consistently influences how history is seen through the eyes of humans over time. Memory is always influenced by our past and present.

However, due to natural misconceptions, the mind can taint the Memory, and there is a possibility we do not even know the full extent – of the complete truth – of what really happened on July 1 to 3, 1863, in Gettysburg. However, we can still get the "why" and "how" questions from analyzing Memory. Like historiography, Memory is full of biases, different perspectives and viewpoints, and of course, forgetfulness.

The time of the Civil War, giving emphasis on the Battle of Gettysburg is one of the most sought-after historical events in American history. The battle of Gettysburg has been supported both by Memory and the abundance of evidential proof. It helps that historians have documented the Civil War exceptionally well.

Chapter Thirteen
Gettysburg is History

Historiography has given us the ability to understand history through media, popular culture, and education. Throughout the times, the narration of how the Battle of Gettysburg went down has been consistently told. However, with each new historian, they give their own unique perspective on what happened in Gettysburg. Some historians would focus on questions, while others would relate the happenings to myths they would want to prove wrong. The theme of Romanticism is consistent with what the historians have studied.

When the Battle of Gettysburg ended, historians took an interest in it. Most of the information we have on the Battle has been taken from official war reports from the different Union commanding officers. Of course, most are from a Union perspective because they did win the Battle. There was a bit of conflict with this, though, that most historians at that time were actually confederates. It wasn't until the mid to late 1880s that the two sides were able to comfortably talk about what transpired in Gettysburg. Both sides hoped that their story would have a say in history. This caused some people to be skeptical about the historical reports written. By the time this era ended, historians could gain the people's trust because of the core beliefs they had established.

The next era in historiography (1900-1950) was the turning point for how people would understand what happened in Gettysburg. Historians finally started to use more of the War Reports and incorporate the Confederate's view on the event. Historians of this time were able to take care of the different controversies that came up. During this time, the emphasis was on analyzing and questioning what really happened on those three days.

1950 – 1970 was the next era for historiography. In this era, they questioned the idea of the Battle's certainty and its significance, if it really made a difference to the Civil War. Also, the historians made an effort to appeal to the crowd.

.

Chapter Fourteen

The Memory of Gettysburg

The battle of Gettysburg goes by a lot of different phrases, such as "the turning point of the war," "the High-Water Mark of the Confederacy," "the bloodiest battle," and "The Last Invasion." Historians may use these terms, but the media and culture helped spread this among the people. It was their way of romanticizing the event by showing the bravery and heroism that it took to have this battle on the central fields of Pennsylvania. Gary Gallagher says that these stories are what allow us to be influenced by what we see and believe. Instead of focusing on the actual battle, we focus on the meaning of what happened in Gettysburg. It is to tear our attention away from the essence of the struggle, which was that it was a fight against slavery.

Today, culture and media greatly influence how people think and understand information. For example, in the world of film, the Civil War was the inspiration for multiple movies just as "Birth of a Nation," "Gettysburg," and "Gone With The Wind." These movies established themes of reconciliation and honor between the Union and the Confederate soldiers, even though that was not true in authentic history.

But remembering Gettysburg on a lighter note does not stop at Hollywood Lane. People have written books about this historical event, such as "The Killer Angels" by Michael Shaara. There were also paintings made by Dale Gallon, Don Troiani, and Mort Kunstler.

Michael Shaara's novel, which was published in 1974, was one of the most popular books on the battle of Gettysburg. The book helps the readers follow the battle story through the perspective of the different army leaders such as Robert Lee, James Longstreet, and Joshua Chamberlain. This novel is reasonably accurate to history; it hones in on the war's crucial moments that give the whole battle's narrative. Shaara zeroed in on

Colonel Joshua Chamberlain's 20th Maine Regiment and their contribution to the Union's plans on the second day of fighting. He was also able to focus on Pickett's raid on the center of the Union line on the last day of battle. He showed this through the eyes of courage and bravery. And if that wasn't a challenge enough, he wanted the readers to understand both sides.

Because of this novel, he helped make a contemporary awareness of Gettysburg and gave the masses a newfound appreciation for the battle of Gettysburg and the Civil War in general.

Chapter Fifteen
Abraham Lincoln's Address

When Abraham Lincoln, the president of America at that time, went to Gettysburg for his address, he was accompanied by Mr. Seward, his Secretary of State: Mr. Usher, his Secretary of the Interior, and Mr. Blair, his Postmaster-General, Mr. John G.

Nicolay, his private secretary, and Colonel John Hay, his assistant private secretary. The French Minister, M. Mercier, the Italian Minister, M. Bertinatti, and several other legation secretaries accompanied him as well. He went to Gettysburg by a special train that brought him right up to the historic site.

Gettysburg was a small town that was slowly becoming known due to the number of visitors it had drawn in. That evening in the town was far from quiet due to the buzz of what would happen the next day during Lincoln's address. Lincoln gave a short speech in the crowd:

"I appear before you, fellow citizens, merely to thank you for this compliment. The inference is a very fair one that you would hear me for a little while at least, were I to commence to make a speech. I do not appear before you for the purpose of doing so, and for several substantial reasons. The most substantial of these is that I have no speech to make. In my position it is somewhat important that I should not say any foolish things. It very often happens that

the only way to help it is to say nothing at all. Believing that is my present condition this evening, I must beg of you to excuse me from addressing you further."

The next day came up, and they all prepared for Lincoln's address:

"Four score and seven years ago our fathers brought forth, upon this continent, a new nation, conceived in liberty, and dedicated to the proposition that all men are created equal.

Now we are engaged in a great civil war, testing whether that nation, or any nation so conceived, and so dedicated, can long endure. We are met on a great battlefield of that war. We come to dedicate a portion of it, as a final resting place for those who died here, that the nation might live. This we may, in all propriety do.

But, in a larger sense, we cannot dedicate, we cannot consecrate, we cannot hallow, this ground The brave men, living and dead, who struggled here, have hallowed it, far above our poor power to add or detract. The world will little note, nor long remember what

we say here; while it can never forget what they did here.

It is rather for us, the living, we here be dedicated to the great task

remaining before us that, from these honored dead we take

increased devotion to that cause for which they here, gave the last

full measure of devotion that we here highly resolve these dead

shall not have died in vain; that the nation, shall have a new birth

of freedom, and that government of the people, by the people, for

the people, shall not perish from the earth."

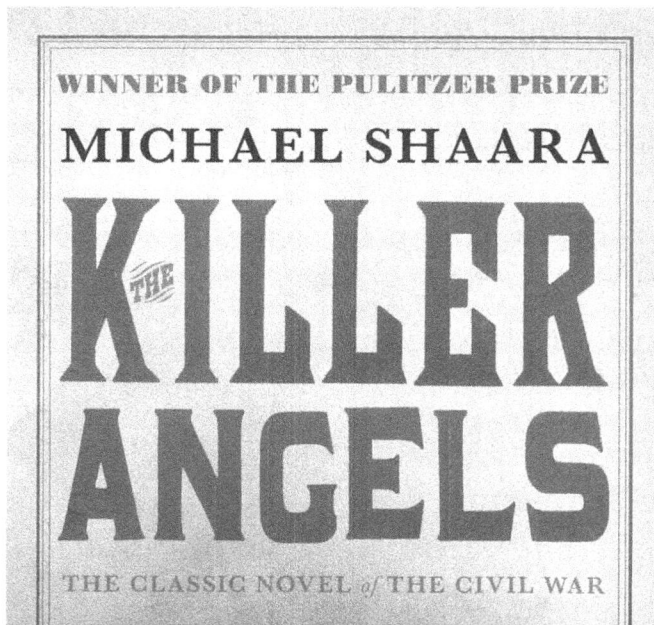

This is the book cover of Killer Angels by Michael Shaara.

This is a picture of President Abraham Lincoln.

Chapter Sixteen
Honoring the Fallen

Mr. Wills requested for the cemetery to be consecrated, and Governor Curtin approved his request. Mr. Wills oversaw the consecration ceremony, and the other governors from other States chipped in to pay their proper respects to the fallen soldiers. Hon. Edwards Everett of Massachusetts was chosen to be the orator for this ceremony. Mr. Wills said in his note to Hon. Everett:

"The several States having soldiers in the Army of the Potomac, who fell at the battle of Gettysburg in July last, gallantly fighting for the Union, have made arrangements here for the exhuming of all their dead, and their removal and decent burial in a cemetery selected for that purpose on a prominent part of the battle-field. The design is to bury all in common, marking with headstones, with the proper inscription, the known dead, and to erect a

suitable monument to the memory of all these brave men, who have thus sacrificed their lives on the altar of their country.

This burial ground will be consecrated to this sacred and holy purpose on Thursday, the 23rd day of October next, with appropriate ceremonies, and the several States interested have united in the selection of you to deliver the oration on that solemn occasion. I am therefore instructed by the governors of the different States interested in the project to invite you cordially to join them in the ceremonies, and to deliver the oration for the occasion."

After sending this, Hon. Everett responded to Mr. Wills:

"I have received your favor of the 23d instant, inviting me, on behalf of the governors of the States interested in the preparation of a cemetery for the soldiers who fell in the great battles of July last, to deliver an address at the consecration. I feel much complimented by this request, and would cheerfully undertake the performance of a duty at once so interesting and honorable. It is,

however, wholly out of my power to make the requisite preparation by the 23rd of October. I am under engagements which will occupy all my time from Monday next to the 1 2th of October, and, indeed, it is doubtful whether, during the whole month of October, I shall have a day at my command.

The occasion is one of great importance, not to be dismissed with a few sentimental or patriotic. It will demand as full a narrative of the events of the three important days as the limits of the hour will admit, and some appropriate discussion of the political character of the great struggle, of which the battle of Gettysburg is one of the most momentous incidents. As it will take me two days to reach Gettysburg, and it will be highly desirable that I should have at least one day to survey the battle-field, I cannot safely name an earlier time than the 19th of November."

After coordinating with other people and inviting the people needed and wanted on this occasion, it was then set that the ceremony would take place on November 19.

The people who attended were President Lincoln, his secretaries, other people from his official retinue, General Schenck, General Stahel, General Stoneman, and their staff, and a number of other officers from the military.

The program at the consecration ceremony was as follows:

- Music by Borgfield's Band.
- Prayer by Rev. T. H. Stockton, D.D. Music by the Marine Band.
- Oration by Hon. Edward Everett.
- Music, Hymn composed by B. B. French, Esq. Dedicatory Remarks by the President of the United States.
- Dirge sang by the choir selected for the occasion.
- Benediction by Rev. H. L. Baugher, D.D.

This is Hon. Edward Everett, the man who officiated the consecration of the Cemetery.

Chapter Seventeen
Conclusion

It is safe to say that the Battle of Gettysburg has been more than just memorable but also valuable to the lives of Americans. But because of its military nature, two of the sections discussed earlier should be reiterated because that is where you will realize the importance of Gettysburg. Reading about it in a narrative and chronologically correct manner is just the first step to really knowing and honoring the memory of the battle at Gettysburg fully.

If you remember the discussion in section two, which is about the different ways you could look at the historical event, you would see that it is more than just one way of seeing the battle. What you must know is that in history, mostly if it is rooted in the military theme, you must know that it is not enough only to see it through the eyes of a civilian. Because the civilians are not the main characters of that story. It is the soldiers. So, to fully understand the story of the battle at Gettysburg, you must look at it from the perspective of its main character: the soldiers. And in that section, you would notice there are two types of militaristic ways to look at that event: the eyes of a strategist and the eyes of a soldier. What you must remember is that even though there is one main character in a story, they still can wear different "hats" like any human being. This means that a person can see things differently at the same time. Have you ever seen a fight and understood both sides of the story? That is what it means to wear different "hats." What is the main point of this is that, when you look at any story, may it be historical or fiction, you must always remember to see it not only from the side character's point of view (because some people do that to be unique) but also through the main character's perspective because they are the main character for a reason. Also, remember that humans are complex, so being able to see through the main character's eyes while knowing the hats they wear is a skill that is hard to achieve but nevertheless can be achieved.

The next section where you can find a key takeaway is section three, where it was discussed how people remember Gettysburg or basically anything that has a story. But let us focus on the battle of Gettysburg. People romanticize this event. Why? There are many reasons, and it is hard to name just a few. But, what you must learn from this section is that just because something is remembered fondly does not mean that it should be. Media today has made almost everything into a sort of fairytale, but it shouldn't be. You must always remember to find the truth in a story and not just focus on the good things about it. Remember: stories are where you can learn something; it is not only for entertainment purposes.

In summary, what are the takeaways you must have from this reading is never to disregard the main person of the story because they are the main character for a reason. Also, knowing the character means knowing the different ways they see something. So remember to always look out for the different hats you can wear in particular stories or arguments. And you must also remember to look for the lesson of the story and not just the fairytale-like elements in them. Do all this, and for sure, you'll be able to analyze events and stories in ways you could have only imagined.

Chapter Eighteen

Discussion Question

Turning points in history are characterized by how much it turns the tide, whether in favor or not of a certain person or group of people. The Battle of Gettysburg was a turning point in American Civil War history. From your experience, what do you think was the turning point for you in your life?

Discussion Question

"Wrong place, wrong time." This quote can be described through this event. The Confederates and the Unions accidentally met each other in Gettysburg. Have you ever experienced a moment when this phrase was very applicable?

Discussion Question

The Confederates were for slavery and forced labor. Why do you think they would believe in such things? Do you think you can ever accept this concept in your life right now?

Discussion Question

In war, you must have defensive and offensive strategies. The Confederates focused on the offensive, and the Unions focused on the defensive. What do you think is better to prioritize? Why?

Discussion Question

The Unions had a strong defensive plan, and the Confederates focused on the offensive. Do you think the Unions won because they had a good defensive strategy or because the Confederates had a bad offensive strategy? Did you think the Confederates became too complacent after the first day?

Discussion Question

The battle of Gettysburg is remembered both solemnly and fondly. In your opinion, how do you want to perceive this historic event? Why do you say that?

Discussion Question

The battle of Gettysburg has been used in the media as inspiration for their outputs. Do you think this is a good way to remember Gettysburg? Or is it better to learn history through historical narratives like in textbooks?

Discussion Question

When President Lincoln came to Gettysburg to give his address, he also went to attend the consecration ceremony of the cemetery. Do you believe it was right to have this ceremony? Why or why not?

Chapter Nineteen
Quiz Question

1. **True/False:** The Union States separated themselves from the Confederates because they did not agree with their thoughts on slavery. The Unions don't believe in slavery, but the Confederates do. So these states are South Carolina, Mississippi, Florida, Alabama, Georgia, Louisiana, Texas, Virginia, Arkansas, Tennessee, and North Carolina.

2. **True/False:** The battle of Gettysburg stretched out for three days. It started on July 1 and ended on July 3. The battle may have been short, but it was costly.

3. **True/False:** The Confederates seemed to be winning on the first day of the battle. However, in the next two days, the Unions started to win. This is due to their good defensive strategy called "the Fish Hook."

4. **True/False:** The battle of Gettysburg has influenced many fictional stories both in film and literature. One of the books

is called "The Killer Angels." This book was written by Robert Lee, a general from the Gettysburg battle himself.

5. **True/ False:** The terrain didn't mean much to the battle. Military strategists did not take them into account when they planned their attacks. The only use for the terrain was its ground, so they had a place to do battle.

6. **True/False:** Women civilians from Gettysburg share many differences with the Union women as well as the Confederate women outside of Gettysburg. However, they have similarities as well. This just shows that they aren't as different as we all would think.

7. **True/False:** The Unions and the Confederates are different in many ways. One is that they are also distinguished by their geographical location. The Unions are from the North, while the Confederates are from the South.

8. **True/ False:** President John F. Kennedy gave the famous Gettysburg address after the battle. He said it during a consecration ceremony that happened in their cemetery. It was to honor the fallen soldiers.

Quiz Answer

1. False. The Confederates separated themselves, not the Union States.

2. True

3. True

4. :False. Lee was a general, yes. But he was not an author. The author was Michael Shaara.

5. False. Terrain played an important role in the strategists' plans.
6. True

7. True

8. False. The President then was Abraham Lincoln.

Bibliography

- **Images:**
- "Union soldiers heading to the battlefield" by San Diego Shooter is licensed under CC BY-NC-ND 2.0. To view a copy of this license, visit https://creativecommons.org/licenses/by-nd-nc/2.0/jp/?ref=openverse.
- "Confederate Monument - SW frieze - Arlington National Cemetery - 2011" by Tim Evanson is licensed under CC BY-SA 2.0. To view a copy of this license, visit https://creativecommons.org/licenses/by-sa/2.0/?ref=openverse.
- "Devil's Den" by Spherical Bull is licensed under CC BY-NC-ND 2.0. To view a copy of this license, visit https://creativecommons.org/licenses/by-nd-nc/2.0/jp/?ref=openverse.
- "Devil's Den" by Spherical Bull is licensed under CC BY-NC-ND 2.0. To view a copy of this license, visit https://creativecommons.org/licenses/by-nd-nc/2.0/jp/?ref=openverse.
- "Michael Shaara: The Killer Angels" by Wolf Gang is licensed under CC BY-SA 2.0. To view a copy of this license, visit https://creativecommons.org/licenses/by-sa/2.0/?ref=openverse.
- "Abraham Lincoln" by casually cruel is licensed under CC BY-NC-ND 2.0. To view a copy of this license, visit https://creativecommons.org/licenses/by-nc-nd/2.0/?ref=openverse.

- "The Hon. John Bell and the Hon. Edward Everett, nominated for President and Vice-President, by the Union Convention at Baltimore, on May 9th, 1860" by exit78 is marked with Public Domain Mark 1.0. To view the terms, visit https://creativecommons.org/publicdomain/mark/1.0/?ref=openverse.

REFERENCES

- Doyle, P. (2006). Military geology and the Battle of Gettysburg, July 1863. *Geology Today*, 22(4), 142-149.
- Dietrich, G. (2021). The Way We Remember It: The Popular Memory of the Battle of Gettysburg.
- Hage, A. A. (1963). The Battle of Gettysburg as Seen by Minnesota Soldiers. *Minnesota History*, 38(6), 245-257.
- Ericson, C. L. (1996). *" The World Will Little Note Nor Long Remember": Women and Gender in the Battle of Gettysburg*(Doctoral dissertation).
- Tilberg, F. (1950). *Gettysburg National Military Park, Pennsylvania* (No. 9). National Park Service.
- Burrage, H. S. (1906). *Gettysburg and Lincoln: The Battle, the Cemetery, and the National Park*. GP Putnam's Sons.
- Weber, J. L. and Hassler,. Warren W. (2022, October 18). *American Civil War. Encyclopedia Britannica.* https://www.britannica.com/event/American-Civil-War
- The Gettysburg Address by Abraham Lincoln. (n.d.). Retrieved November 23, 2022, from https://www.abrahamlincolnonline.org/lincoln/speeches/gettysburg.htm

Bonus Downloads

*Get Free Books with **Any Purchase**History Encounters*

Every purchase comes with a FREE download!

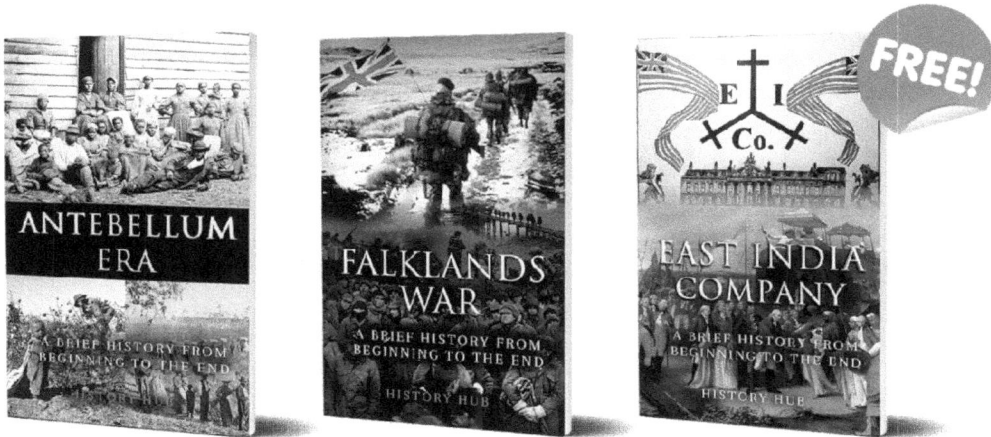

Thank You For Reading

As an independent publisher

with a tiny marketing budget

we rely on readers, like you.

If you're receiving help from this book,

would you please take a moment to write a brief review?

We really appreciate it.

Milton Keynes UK
Ingram Content Group UK Ltd.
UKHW031142081224
452079UK00012B/105

9 798330 613380